AB

D1589123

Selected Poems 1972 – 1997

for Jean and Tom Brooks
with love

Selected Poems
1972 – 1997

Michael Schmidt

Smith/Doorstop Books

Published 1997 by
Smith/Doorstop Books
The Poetry Business
The Studio
Byram Arcade
Westgate
Huddersfield HD1 1ND

ISBN 1 869961 82 X

British Library Cataloguing-in-Publication Data. A catalogue record
for this book is available from the British Library.

Typeset at The Poetry Business
Printed by Peepal Tree, Leeds
Distributed by Password (Books) Ltd.,
23 New Mount Street, Manchester M4 4DE

Cover design by Blue Door Design, Heckmondwike
Picture by Urs Lüthi
Wine label used by permission of Coop Suisse, Bâsle
Photograph by Stephen Raw

The author and publishers thank Anvil Press Poetry for permission
to reprint work from Michael Schmidt's several collections.

The Poetry Business acknowledges the help of the Arts Council of
England, Kirklees Metropolitan Council and Yorkshire & Hum-
berside Arts.

CONTENTS

from *Desert of the Lions*

Scorpion

for John Schmidt

Under its stone, it pleats
and unpleats ebony, it digs
a bed which is a body-print
exactly, room for pincer, tail
and sting. If it elbows out, it leaves
cold accurate evidence of its tenancy.

Bedded with it, less precise,
the ambling grubs and slow-worms
eat and burrow deep sometimes
as earthworms, not disturbing that
fast eel of their element – for it
has eyes or nerves that flinch

malignantly at a grain's shift.
I follow you hunting with jar and trowel,
with gloves, this poison tail.
Each time you turn the right stone up –
warm flat stones which roof
an airless square of dark

and hold all night the sun's warmth
for the black king-pin of the poor soil.
The stone raised, the creature poises
tense and cocked. Tail curled, it edges
forward, edges backward – its enemy
so big he is invisible (though a child)

hunched over it, who trembles too
at such a minute potency.
And you flick it with the trowel
into the jar, where it jerks and flings
its fire in all directions at hard
transparency. It asks no mercy.

You bear it to an anthill,
tip it on the dust. Like a cat
it drops right side up, into a tide
of sharp red pincers. It twitches
its tail to a nicety and twice
stings itself – to death. Piece by piece

it is removed underground by the ants –
a sort of burial – perhaps to be
reassembled as a kingly effigy
somewhere deeper than we care to think
bound homeward with our empty jar:
and the field, full of upturned stones.

Away

He left the room abruptly
dreaming, on a horse.
Still in bed of course
he rode, rode to the sea.

Behind him, his life strung
mile-lengths of wire back
over sand to a shack
where a telephone rang

unanswered. At the sea-side
water made no sound.
Deaf conches strewed the sand.
Seabirds on still air rode

above giant turtles, thick
headed, like fists or a thought.
Silence caught:
the rider could not come back.

His wife murmured in sleep
a dream he did not own.
In its moon-cradle his sin
slept its tiny clenched sleep.

The sea, silent and plain,
lay like a field of weed.
He dismounted and did
what a man will do in pain.

He took off coat and shirt.
He took off skin and bone.
He spread them out on stone:
rose, hyacinth, and heart.

Underwater

Underwater, this is the cathedral
sea. Diving, our bubbles rise
as prayers are said to do, and burst
into our natural atmosphere–
occupying, from this perspective,
the position of a heaven.

The ceiling is silver, and the air
deep green translucency. The worshippers
pray quietly, wave their fins.
You can see the colour of their prayer
deep within their throats: scarlet, some,
and some fine-scaled vermilion; others

pass tight-lipped with moustaches
trailing and long paunches, though
they are almost wafer-thin seen sideways,
or unseen except for whiskers.
Further down, timorous sea-spiders
slam their doors, shy fish disappear

into their tenement of holes, and eels
warn that they have serpent tails.
Deep is wild, with beasts one meets
usually in dreams. Here the giant octopus
drags in its arms. We meet it.
We are hungry in the upper air, and you

have the sea-spear that shoots deep;
you fire accurately, raising a conflagration
of black ink. The animal grabs stone
in slow motion, pulls far under a ledge
and piles the loose rock there as if
to hide might be enough. It holds tight,

builds sanctuary, and I think cries
'sanctuary!' It dies at your second shot.
We come aboveboard then, with our eight-armed
dinner and no hunger left, pursued by the bland
eyes of fish that couldn't care, by black
water and the death we made there.

11

'Indian-Pipes are Flowers'

at the Desierto de los Leones

In this sort of forest, the bent
pink Indian-pipes all day in drizzle
are puffing mist; and through pines,
as if on damp fire, the monastery smokes,
tall above catacombs, black,
moss-grown, with absent bells.

Monks took the choice spots,
but sent to Spain reports of arid
desert retreats, implying dangerous lions
were about. This desert provided
ample peace to bring off Inquisitions
without prurient eyes. Here, bound,

Indians who could not say the Creed
were brought for instruction, with them
their mild gods of furrow, maize –
exorcised, and only the birds knew.
Indian bones were buried always outside
consecrated ground, not deep.

Those monks learned to construct
a garden where they could relax
after the arduous duties of faith:
zinnia, primula, chrysanthemum and rose
run wild now with a native inspiration,
but then were trellised, chastised into flower.

Within the outlying buildings where we walk
stand posts of body-height,
cut with marks of rope. Minute red poppies
everywhere, recent, like blood-seed,
are spilled, reeking of earth –
the bones of rodents too.

Indians don't come now to pick
mushrooms or sleep in the ghostly lap
of this pine forest – only
vesper swallows home to silence.
Monks preferred the birds to anything.

The Well At Balankanche

Spit down this long well-
shaft sounds like a drum-beat,
deep. Water is stone-dark
down there, stone still.
Even the graves we dig don't
go so close to silence.

The Indians nowadays still
put jade pearls in one another's
mouths and leap from high
well-lips like this to reach
'the bone and body of night' –
not here, but north among

the churchless thicket of Kabah.
We salvage their ancestors
by dredging: bone and moss,
beads, clay figurines. Two hands
bound still with threads
of sisal rope we brought up –

took a cast of them before
they dried to dust. I wonder
how they feel, hand in hand,
when water snaps
over their heads and takes
their pearls, lets them

bound together drift to ledges
deeper than our thought,
to lie forever touching, touched
by blind fish and minute fresh
water crab. Bone on bone,
prayed to and envied by the tribe.

We people of the upper air:
our sacrifice of spit is all
the water claims of us. We steal
its pearls and analyse its bones.
It clots our pumps each day
with blue-gilled, eyeless fish.

from *My Brother Gloucester*

The Judas Fish

I wake to this bewilderment –
my porthole's gone under, the sea flows
too high tonight, and trickles in.
It is not rain, but wind that lifts
and leaves it hovering.

Moments pass without the sky at all.
I share the water-dark that is a sound
intimately chilling, like a voice that whispers
from the world a charm into a dream.
Through the latched porthole

the gentle bleeding from the sea
will be tomorrow a salt web across the floor.
I light my lamp against the starless voice.
It is my face that looks me in the eye.
I cup my hands, look closer

through the face into a shallow pool of light.
A fish might take the porthole for a mild
luminous fish-eye; a night diver
might spot it from a distance as a coin,
antique, the frail imperial face

on alloyed gold, wide-eyed,
not negotiable, gazing
into the marches around empire
where froth is the untouchable barbarian.
Looking out, indeed, there is not much to see,

no diver, no near fish, nothing
to crave possession over,
though there is a strange
possessiveness in water, as in sunlight,
determining the shadows. Water casts up

shadows of a curious kind, swirling
three inches from the eyes – an impulse
to undo the latch for once, gingerly
to invite oblivion in,
let the driving current touch and have its way.

Yet it is a driven current at the pane
that has claimed as many histories as time
and planted them in beds of sand and coral,
in thicket weeds, in feeding of its fish;
its fluid memory retains suspended

elements of mountains, ships and mariners
unredeemable as salt within the blood,
but present: the dead are tasted
like rich sediment, flooding
secret latitudes.

Subsiding with the wind the water goes,
my porthole fills with constellations
that never touched a life,
and they are welcome, identifiable –
although before they came back I believe

a fish pulsed into view in the dwindling water
with thirty silver scales upon its side
and a Judas eye trained on me, focusing.
I slipped the latch then.
It was starlight that came in.

Writing

for Benedict Schmidt

The cone-snail shrinks from us.
Its mouth is sealed.
Nothing will tempt it out again
but washing in the sea. It is cast up.
We gather it with shells and take it home.

Of all that we collected it is this
we look at first. It's edged with tiny stings.
We set it on the floor
and bring the reading glass to make it large.
It leaks a yellow liquid like a wound.

In the lip: a rim of glyphs.
They are crimson on pearl white, each
distinctly written, like a text we magnify.
These tendril lines are veins
that bear poison to the stings.

If we knew how to read
we could not deny a language here.
The fluent tracery is more
than a snail articulating vanity:
it is a charm to keep its body whole.

An eyeless thing
fingering with blunt horns
the walls it grew, gradually
sketched these images,
translating them by instinct into shell;

it was a jelly substance working sand,
fitting itself to sand and sand to it,
observing the reciprocal slow laws
to make its long vault issue from the heart
up to the lips and there describe these symbols.

We cannot pry open the fixed mouth.
Does the writing continue in the throat,
through the length of the deep whorl, until
at the core the riddle is resolved?
We tap it. It fractures like egg-shell.

In the innermost recess the snail has shrivelled
hard as a pea. We are deceived:
the vaults are white throughout,
and what there was to say was clearly
written on the lips and spoken there.

Words

after Hofmannsthal

Child, your eyes will darken soon with wonder –
and darken ignorantly till they're blind.
We will pass by you as we were passed by.

The fruit is bitter. It will sweeten in the dark
and drop into your hands with broken wings.
Cherish it a day. But it will die.

The wind comes down to you from history.
It chilled us too. The phrases it repeats
are stale with pleasure, stale with punishment.

The paths lead from the garden to the world,
to places where light burns among the trees
that raise their wings but cannot hope to fly.

Who cast the root of everything so deep
that nothing flies away that we can name?
Why can we laugh and in a moment cry

and give a name to laughter and to tears?
What is the illness that our eyes grow dark?
– We are men because we are alone:

we touch and speak, but silence follows words
the way a shadow does, the hand draws back.
The curtain blows and there is no one there.

What removed you to this solitude,
into this common light, this common twilight?
It is that word, twilight, that called you down –

a word the wind has handed on to us
undeciphered, and it might be love –
rich with a honey pressed from hollow combs.

20

My Town

for Isabel Schmidt

It is as though the whole town is on ice.
Skaters with a speed of birds
greet each other on reflected cloud
mid-stream, up-stream, past the crippled boats.
There is a horse and sledge.
A bonfire burns its censer shape into the cold.
Someone sells grilled fish

again today, for it's been weeks
the river froze, and a man dared
walk out on the water.
No one has looked back since:
ice-fishermen with saw and string,
the schools of children, the slower
shopkeepers like large sedate fish.

The habitual town has ceased. It's chosen
another better world, a world of days
prayed for, persistent beyond hope,
a flowering of impossibilities.
Buildings line the shore
derelict like plundered sea-chests
and the pirate is the ice.

I tie on my skates and find the air
moves me like a feather from the shore.
I leave town for the frozen falls.
I fly up-stream like a salmon, light
with spawn. I come home
and pass by for the sea, and turn again.
Sun sparks my blades, I send up

grit of ice like quick flame.
I burn my hours religiously,
my ceremony to the ice and air.
But today the air is warmer, our days
are numbered. The falls are dripping
and the sea barks and barks
into the brittle river mouth. It is like

21

sailing at the end of a brief world, beyond
responsibility, and time is purposeless,
pure of daily history and bread.
To put on wings is an authentic dream, and yet
up on shore the dirtied nest of facts
is patient in the sun, tall and lowering
above the vistas of the heart,

and even now beneath the ice
the other world continues
undisturbed, the weeds are spun by currents,
the pearls increase to buy our future eyes;
the small fish feed, are fed on, the great
round-eyed flounder old as water
subsist on certainties among stilled keels
and out to sea, by rough boulders and the light,
the wrecked laden hulls, the mariners ...

If the inhabitants of that world look up
they perceive hairline cracks
fissuring the ice
and our veined shadows pass
against the light like baits
they will not take, but wait –
cold acolytes, whose business is
each candle and the dark.

The Fool

I warn you, said the Fool,
I have a job to do. I do it well.
I am the lowest rung on the man ladder;
my place, unchallenged, is not inconvenient

for I look up and undersee your polished boots
holed through utterly beneath, your hosiery
tattered at the knee, and you in silks outside
below are bare as apricots, as radishes.

Your bodies' downward scent is unperfumed.
I smell your misdemeanours and your motives.
– Yet every heart beats only from my heart
if it beats truly, though no voice speaks

my language. None speaks truly.
In my rhetoric I am in the earth the undertaker,
the first worm who bears the licensed key
and unlocks every body: mine

is the first taste, my certificate
implies a corpse impure enough to plunder.
I am the deepest, oldest, thinnest fish
upon the seabed in the rocks and sand:

I see the world entire in glancing up,
I intercept and touch the whale's long sound,
the prim sea-horse I watch grow old and faithless,
the sallow bladder-fish inflate and fawn

on sleek sea-kale trees that stand up like kings.
And yet I have no name but my two eyes,
my speech that none replies to,
a venerable, antique uniform.

I have – I'm had on sufferance.
I am afraid of dark as much as you.
I pull my cap across my eyes and sleep.
I dream of an ignorant and sunny kingdom

trivial, passionate, where all have hearts
within undisfigured bodies that are breathing
like men and women coming out of marble
into an actual day, as fish move out from weeds

blinking at the galleons that sink
and break before them on the seabed, spilling
treasure meaningless and brilliant, habitable;
and the drowned mariners more slowly drifting
touch down as gently dead as leaves.

The English Lesson

after Pasternak

When it was Desdemona's turn to sing
and only minutes of her life remained,
she did not mourn her star, that she had loved:
she sang about a tree, a willow tree.

When it was Desdemona's time to sing,
her voice grew deeper, darker as she sang;
the darkest, coldest demon kept for her
a weeping song of streams through rough beds flowing.

And when it was Ophelia's turn to sing
and only minutes of her life remained,
she was dry as light, as a twig of hay:
wind blew her from the loft into the storm.

And when it was Ophelia's time to sing,
her dreams were waning, all but the dream of death.
Bitter and tired – what tokens sank with her?
In her hair wild celandine, and willows in her arms.

Then letting fall the rags of human passion,
heart-first they plunged into the flowing dark,
fracturing their bodies like white tinder,
silencing their unbroken selves with stars.

The Sleigh

after a theme of Turgenev, for Charles Schmidt

The colours have gone out.
It is like death – blind white
and the sun is white: we speed
the way we always wished –
a sleigh, the harness bells – across the snow.

It's not what we expected.
Afraid on the ice road
we ring to the empty farms
that we've come their way but not to stop.
Who set the burning pennies on our eyes?

Think – if the runners struck a rut
and hurled us into temporary graves
face-down like heretics; or if the jingling
ceased and we flew silently
on into the open throat of night.

Speed and the snow
blend field and hedge and landmark
in one whiteness like a future.
Perhaps the thaw will turn it up like new –
and yet we cannot see that far today.

Under the arcane dunes
suppose the past is unreclaimable
too truly for March sun and its tired miracle.
What if a half-hearted wish for warmth
is all we bring ourselves, and bring no love

hot to melt the things it cannot love?
What if we trust all changes to the snow?
I think the snow will see us off:
we're going to die
whirling, two flakes

of headlong colour
over the unmarked brink.
In a flash of white, as though we are to hang,
we shall relive our separate short lives.
    – We have not touched or taken

the feather weight of pain.
If it was war, then we were traitors there.
If it was famine, we ate on and on; and now
we're turned to cowards in a day we owned,
returned as serfs to fields we ruled as czars,

we plough the snow where once
we led the hunt through hedge and stream-bed
up to the lodge and there were ladies there.
It is neglect and snow leave open graves
we ride from to worry at a world

we partly chose, and where
forgetfulness makes easy graves we go
across a brilliance like purity
to no known place.
The driver turns and points but we are blind.

I dread a destination and the thaw
that will set us down and leave us to ourselves
as we are now. We are
the dying penitent who feels too late
the cold breath of the beggar on his hand.

I wish I could look on
rather than be here a piece of blindness.
I would not call
to those who go together
and seem upon the snow as cold as snow,

but from a distant cottage I would watch
a tiny horse advance
with a faint pulse of bells
drawing its burden, as a spider draws a fly
across its web of light into the dark.

Natalya's Dream

for N.E. Gorbanevskaya,
detained in prison mental hospital

Her heart peers out
between her breathing shoulder-blades:
curious, fist-sized.

It gazes down the spine
as down a highway. From its high vantage
it observes unbroken snow,

the broken slumber, broken snow.
Under glacial contours of the skin
the lakes persist, dilate; the rivers

irrigate so deep cartographers ignore them.
Aya, Raya, her Estonian names
conjure their villages,

the farmers who received her
in their houses and their language:
how they are squinting,

blinded by their fields of snow,
how the one road leads
one way and loses them.

There, at the highway's end,
Tartu, a pole of exile.
Here, between the shoulders,

the other pole of exile is the heart –
renewing the old journeys
with each syllable of pulse –

until it flickers like a candle, votive,
ignited to the guardian of exiles,
shadowed out by the twin blades of bone.

She wakes to the ward smell
and sound of other dreaming,
in a frayed prison smock, in the early light;

to her face reflected from the dusty pane:
a face of Russia with no caption, with no
black border, no number and no name.

Wasps' Nest

It was the fruit I wanted, not the nest.
The nest was hanging like the richest fruit
against the sun. I took the nest

and with it came the heart, and in my hand
the kingdom and the queen, frail surfaces,
rested for a moment. Then the drones

awoke and did their painful business.
I let the city drop upon the stones.
It split to its deep palaces and combs.

It bled the insect gold,
the pupa queens like tiny eyes
wriggled from their sockets, and somewhere

the monarch cowered in a veil of wings
in passages through which at evening
the labourers had homed,

burdened with silence and the garden scents.
The secret heart was broken suddenly.
I, to whom the knowledge had been given,

who was not after knowledge but a fruit,
remember how a knot of pains
swelled my hand to a round nest;

blood throbbed in the hurt veins
as if an unseen swarm mined there.
The nest oozed bitter honey.

I swaddled my fat hand in cotton.
After a week pain gave it back to me
scarred and weakened, a shrivelled skin.

A second fruit is growing on the tree.
Identical – the droning in the leaves.
It ripens. I have another hand.

28

The Freeze

We can't sleep tonight. The ice has formed –
from thin skin at evening
to deep stone. With midnight
the boat's aground in it.
Planks shriek against the hardening.

Below deck a film of frost pales everything.
Our breath makes beads of ice. We pace
between the hatch and bunks.
The world would end by ice
tonight, for sure, if we lay down.

Come outside: the wind has sculpted
sails to marble drapery;
on the line our laundry freezes to
a rigor mortis of our bodies' clothes.
Night will hardly darken all this glass –

the stars are treble on its rippled plane.
Birds stiffen on the surface,
bellies up, like fish.
We started from a tropic on whose shore
the lizards' tongues were flames of malachite

in leaves that trailed on to the tide,
and crimson fish were couriers there
to caverns where eels uncoiled their sting.
Night plankton burned our wake –
for years we have been heading north.

When lips are tucked away for good
and rigid as ice-starched shirt and trousers
we pass the climax of our slow miasma,
and the river hardens in the arteries
till the heart with the hull surrenders

to stillness and is broken like a stone;
when our histories are minuted, adjourned,
our faces upturned to a Sabbath star,
this will be the scene if we can see,
the fish arrested with the drifting tyres,

the dry snow driven into dunes of ash.
It was not like this in the other place –
there all was fire and water,
nothing stilled the waves
that might be furious though they never died

to the intolerable vacancy
we pace to keep the blood awake. Come down.
We'll light the burner, thaw our fingers out.
We are the ashes that will cover us,
our inch of life, our mile, our field of breathing.

from *A Change of Affairs*

A Dream

for C. H. Sisson

I had a dream on good authority
That fastened on me like a stitch in skin:
Construct a boat, God said, *along these lines*
And spread the plan out on his cloudy knee.

So many cubits wide, and here the masts,
And make the hull as large as a hotel.
The animals, of course. Reptiles? and bugs?
Each animal, and two of those in love.

There will be forty nights without a star
And forty days go by without a sun
And when the clouds break there will be nowhere
Till oceans find another Hemisphere.

That dream is some time past. The fields are full
Of grain, the mating creatures now give birth.
I come home evenings a puzzled man,
Hearing the infants cry, touching the solid earth.

I tell the dream and reason thus with Shem:
'Dear boy,' I say, 'if we construct this thing
The flood may come and we will be the cause.
God does not act until his will is done.'

'The earth will all be ours, though,' says Shem:
'Imagine, all the ground from here to night,
And God will fix his eye on us alone
And make our offspring rich, our furrows full.'

Japheth is lazy. When I worry him
He says, 'Let's have it built, then we can sleep
For forty days under the care of God
And settle later in a quiet grove.'

Ham is a craftsman, handy with a saw.
I hardly told the dream when he began
Pricing old planks and readying his tools.
He worries me, his eye on destiny.

Shem tallies, Japheth dreams, and Ham prepares.
Our neighbours have heard nothing though the wave
Hangs over them and I could make it break.
I don't believe the dream was meant for me.

The Brother

Why is his sacrifice
More suitable than mine?
I give the grain I've sown
And he, sheep from his flock.
Mine is a laboured gift,
His a giving back.

It is not what I give –
Rather, my shape you despise.
You light his flame to see
A body nicely formed
For sitting on a hill
Above a bleating flock
And playing on a reed
A parody of praise.

You make my flame slow
And smokier than light.
My arms and legs are scarred
From moving in sharp grass.
I am no idol for
The god who made the snake
Or the abhorrent tree.
My praise is in the field
Enacting punishment.

If beauty's not my tithe,
But only what I do,
If what I am attracts
No more than a slow flame,
I know what I can kill
To draw your eye to me.

Absalom

It's Absalom who mouths the famous prayer –
'David, David, father, O my father' –
Meanwhile his father king is treading air,
A fist of twigs has clutched him by the hair;
He walks and walks, the tree won't let him down –
It holds the head although it lost the crown.
The air is cooler when the sun has spilled
Its cordial red along the sterile hills,
Imbibed the sweat of battle by degrees,
Leaving the salt, the man, the faithful tree.
The son is victor and his golden hair
Lights like a torch the court's grey atmosphere
And for an evening, mourning victory,
Keeps to the forms of grief with a dry eye.
Perhaps I, David, who once bore the head
Of brute Goliath that my stone struck dead,
And freed my people to their wilderness
And made my body their intelligence –
Beautiful, articulate and just – am now
Only a weariness. I see him grow
Into the shadow that time shed from me
As though it suited him; and from this tree
I worship him as my loves worshipped me;
Desire's old logic in a head that's grey,
Gnarled fingers, and the once eloquent heart
Give way like stone the sharp frost cleaves apart
And leaves. I take my human medicine
And do not curse him, my usurping son,
But close my eyes to hold him in my head –
Here in this tree, his lover, hanging dead.

A Carol

It is a winter sky.
I take a fist of stars –
A hundred if you please –
And seed dark vacancies.

They choose a hundred lands
To throb above.
Each land is cold and yet
Not closed to miracles.

A hundred miracles
Would strain credulity:
If man can love no more
Than once in a blue moon

A God loves his bad world
One time in history
At most, and pours his blood.
He'll come next time as fire.

But in a hundred lands
The shepherds leave their flocks
To seek a manger child
Following my stars.

And in a hundred Easts
The wise men pack their bags
And leave their palaces
And people to the snow.

Each manger's visited.
There's one beneath each star.
There is only one child,
One miracle. One star

Tells the truth and stays.
The others draw their line
And fall into the sea
With their false promises.

The sheep have strayed meanwhile.
The people die of cold.
The shepherds will not stop
Their scrabbling in the straw.

The wise men have not homed.
They wait upon the child
Although he died and rose
Too long ago for love
Except by miracle.

'Until I Built the Wall ...'

Until I built the wall they did not find me.
Sweet anarchy! attending quietly
To wild birds or picking the blackberry.

Trespassers did not know they erred and came
In and away, leaving the land the same.
The hunter went to richer ground for game.

Tending, profitless, my property
Which no map mentioned, where no metal lay
In veins beneath the surface of hard clay

And bristle grass, I watched my livestock – scores
Of lizards, armadillos, and the birds –
Free citizens. I had concealed no snares.

Mere ground. Mere nothing harvested or sown.
But how the shadows made the rough design
Live as a landscape for a man alone!

So I grew proud. That's why I built the wall
Of stone and mortar, and I drove a nail
Into a stake and hung a sign to tell

The wanderer *Private Land*, with guarantees
Of instant death for *anyone who tries*
To enter here: leave hope. Vain promises!

Who would I kill or could I kill?
Before I turned a servant of the will
To mark my ground, indeed, who would I hurt or kill?

Now peering from the rim of my high wall
I see the plain outside abruptly shrill
With enemies I do not know. They call

Who's in there, what do you mean, and why?
I hold my peace, but they've discovered me
Because I drew a line, a *Here am I.*

They rob my peace, they take away my sleep.
Their voices drizzle all the night. I step
Along the wall as round a castle keep

36

Till in the daylight there they stand again,
Drawn up from their shadows till at noon
Ghost warriors hover by the place I own.

As ribs around a heart, the gentle wall
Tucks in the land, or as a crisp snail shell
Cups its soft cause. Yet yearlong vigil

Sours memory of the lovely ground,
Rivets to masonry the heart and hand:
I tend a straitened altitude of stone.

Choice

for S.H.

I am like the worm.
Cut in two, I'd thrive.
Within the metaphor
I greet myself, I take
My right hand in my right
And looking eye to eye
I'm satisfied. I need
A knife to make it true,
A simple slice, and clean;
Another lover too.

The worm resembles me.
The rough dark hardens it.
Within the metaphor
It only knows it is
And not which way it goes
To what, from what, how far.
I want a blade to fall
Between me so I move
Forward fore and aft
And double the odds for love.

The worm and I emerge
Into the rainy light.
We wander on the lawn
And lose our entrances.
I kneel on a flagstone
And press it with my thumb.
It twists into a ring
And writhes away again.
Here resemblance ends
Like casual marriages.

A Change of Affairs

You came at evening,
A tardy labourer,
And joined the courtyard full
Of those I'd called between
The hours of six and six.
You had not touched
The vines or turned the soil,
But at the table where
I paid the equal wage
To those whose skin was burned
By a whole day of sun
And those who came at five,
Whose brows were dry of sweat,
You claimed your salary.

And what is due to you –
To those white hands, that face?
What to that bright dress,
The body with its sweet
Scent among reeking flesh?
I make you stand aside
And when the men are gone
I give you what remains:
The trellises and vines,
The hoes and rakes, the keys.
Next day I come at dawn
To work in the hot sun.

Waking and Sleeping

1

I forget which of these plants I planted.
The wind brought some, a few were in the soil.
Better to dig them up and start again
And know the garden when it comes to flower.

But the seeds – I cannot trust or credit
The words on the bright paper pod.
Inside is a sound like sand – dry, credible.
Better a barren patch than unknown harvest.

A barren patch, burnt off, kept dry as cinders,
Protected against rain and from the dew.
Yet it, like any acre, a night neglected,
And there are toadstools the air has made,

Exotic lungs – a nap will foster them.
Even a desert is not sterile soil.
I will give up the plot, give over
The flower, seed, the lungs, the watching over.

2

Being free I am compelled one way:
Down hill, my will exhausted. I decline
Like water around stones into the sea.
But at the shore I pause in time, I turn
And climb the hill again, compelled one way.

Better than up and down, to be a slave
And take direction from a cunning goad,
Or be a puppet that accepts the strings
And always moves secure in law or pain.
Being free, I would elect that course.

But being free denies me that request
And will not let itself exceed its word.
I have no rule but lawlessness, no heart
Except the motor of my pulse; in sleep
My eyes come loose and roll about my skull
Like pearls. I am the doll of anarchy.

Piano

You can make music come from those cold keys.
Alone and grandly I adjust the stool,
Flap up my shirt tail, take your seat, arrange
Feet on the pedals, poise my hands, then pause.
Around me evening holds its breath.

Accustomed as I am to hear you play,
I hear you with my hands above the keys
And can imagine that I sit apart
Patient, watching your shoulders move
Into the music as a dancer sways,

Your intimacy with a sheet of notes
I can't approach, your feet that press
Gently the brass pedals so they take
A chord as far as you would have it go
Or clear the air of music instantly.

There, your sleeves turned
Up to the elbow, and your forearms pale
Above the ivory and the shadow keys
On evenings like this ... the ghost of you
Compels me to keep silence in your place.

Here and There

There, you are climbing to the Aber Falls.
Here, at my table, I think of you:
The mist around you and your body's pulse
Makes its own intimate atmosphere
From which you gaze out loving that landscape –
You pass the wild horses and the marsh trees.
Here, beside myself, I follow you.

Last year we went that path in rain and found
The falls come out of cloud, not off a cliff:
A torrent poured by the invisible. We took
Shoes and socks off, waded to the pool.
Slipping, letting go, who cares: in deep
Up to the waist, with the fish, we moved
Under the fall's full weight.
The water struck us like an avalanche.

41

The weather never cleared. It won't today.
There, now, you may have reached the upper pool.
You may be taking off your shoes and socks.
Here, I flex my toes inside my shoes.
Shall I go take a bath? I ask you:
How to wash this image out, erase
Trees, the hand in hand, the shaft of water,
Its force that knocked me dumb into your arms?

The Honeysuckle

Your honeysuckle, since you've been away
Breathes heavily. Your room is full of scent.
I look into the dusk. Your labour's there,
The tending that gradually seduced
Soil and stem to render up a pattern.
Your work becomes like theirs, as they reduce
Their straggling to ordered scent and hue,
Hospitable to birds. Your only care
Is measuring of growth, decay; and time
Is seasons of the bud, the withering,
Unabstract, with unspoken promises.

Unbroken, too. Each year the place prepares,
Punished and loved – two passions of one heart –
To give what profit a beloved can give.
You choose that time of year to go,
Leaving to me the climax. I'm not in love
With greenery, but you – and left with what you made
Of a small garden and a broken tree
I fumble with your chores, meek but unbeguiled.

Evening takes off the brilliance by degrees
Until the poppy is a ghost, the rose
A bruise among its foliage; then dark
Fills in the scented trough between the hedges,
Extinguishes the tree, absolves the eye from all
Reality. I lie in your dark room
Intent to think of nothing, sleep.
Only, the honeysuckle comes,
An air that you prepared, to fill your place.

from *Choosing a Guest*

'Under the great stone Churn ...'

Under the great stone Churn with its hoop of shale
That ticks all winter like a giant clock
And sends down sheets of rock a hundred feet
Into our unwalled orchards that stay sweet
With fallen fruit until spring sours them –
Under the Churn I grow up and then old
All in a year, and sit here on the soil
Wrapped like a caterpillar in my rugs
But am unchanged and do not hope to fly.
Only the eye scales the steep air, the ear
Calls down the lonely birds and focuses
In age and silence, in their solitude,
Whatever being has been scattered, multiplied,
And the dropped shale seems written with some news,
The language strange, implicit, that I read
But can translate not even into words.

Neighbouring is the walled yard of the church.
My trees overhang and are drawn down
By green-black ivy so they feed the dead
Red fruit and little leaves, a dust of blossom.
It will not be hard to climb the dry stone wall
And add a life to those four centuries:
My trees send their long heavy branches over
To feel a way for me, and so repay
My care, as they did my father's and his father's:
They are my hands and the dark ivy holds them.

In a Darkening Thicket

My voice lost, the thicket growing dark,
Are they all gone? Only my lips say *Fetch me*.
Night settles, round and perfect as an egg.

If I wave a handkerchief it will be a shadow
Like a bat caught in a web, and there are not even stars
– The gesture of Icarus, his mess of feathers
White on the sea as the foamy cap of a wave.

How far they have moved off – I hear them laughing,
Breaking their ways through, home, in all directions.
No one says *Where is he? He is always slow*,
Or looks over a shoulder into the dark
Calling my name. They are all blind as I
But go together, talking, while I stand
Afraid not of danger or the place,
But my companions receding like a tide.

Brittle the wood when I move against the twigs,
Brittle the match I strike on my shoe
To see the darkness darker round the glow.
I cup the light in my hand against the breeze
And know that they will find me if I touch
This trembling stem and this with fire. How far is home?
Will I see the distant windows in the glare
And my companions wait at the open door?

Adam

Desire stayed with me long after you'd gone.
How long? An hour or two. I went to sleep,
And into sleep it followed me. We followed
Each echoing corridor in search of you.

Desire woke with me and all day it clings
– A shadow cast before which even noon
Does not erase. I pace the long garden
To and fro between box-wood and rose.

I name my little trees, the oak and beech,
The willow, apple, sycamore – all planted close.
I name such blossoms as I know: the lilac,
The honeysuckle with its hint of flesh,

The poppy holding up nine heads, one fractured
Into a flare of red, the others tight still;
Veined irises I name, geum and pansy.
I turn to flowerless plants and name the yew.

Desire has gathered pollen for its use.
Night settles on us in the scented air.
I stand exhausted as after long labour,
Naming each growing thing, not to name you.

Choosing a Guest

Whom shall I invite? The centrepiece
Is five red apples on a walnut dish.
The table takes their sheen. Whom
Shall I invite to what the trees provide?

Before I choose a guest I go outside.
It is evening almost, almost winter here:
Under the apple tree a pungent mud of fruit,
One bough fractured by the wealth it bears.

I have chosen. And will she come?
It is like necromancy to invite
The guest who yesterday, the day before,
Laughing, turned to darkness at my board.

Absence I will invite. I will invite
The morning birds, and I will not ask her.
The birds will not come, and she will not come.
The sheen will pass from fruit into the dark.

It is too late to eat, too late to ask.
I shall say grace but break no bread.
The lamp will not be lit; I shall sit still
As shadow takes the taste instead.

Here is my bed. How the scent of apples
Clings to my breathing, and the scent of her.
I am alarmed
How nothing leaves me, though the light is gone.

New Poems

'Evening, Lancashire ...'

Evening, Lancashire. The tower block
Leans over Blackburn to a swollen hill
Hazed in purple that might become heather
Where lovers tryst. The sky is starred and still.

I like your window, your blue counterpane
Turning to shadow where it swallows you –
One half of you; your famous eyes are glowing
With Lancashire, like rain-damp stone. Untrue.

The heart paces over your lean acres.
The fingers rake your hair. The lips explore
Veins, and taste blood racing through the soil
And curl back to your heart. You're really here

But who you are's uncertain. When I ask,
Each word's a kiss, a sting, a falling star.
You're sorcerer, your spell is glance and hand,
Each kiss a lie, kindling to desire.

Where am I, lying by the side of you,
Suddenly, for some hours? When night breaks,
Even in the dark you're there, and glowing
Even in sleep, unearthly. And you wake

So we go down, we go out to a dance
Where every eye is on you. Who am I,
The satyr with the hunted look, the stranger,
Who wants you another hour, wants to lie

Beside your narrow belly, by your heart
That rattles your tense hand, his stupid heart
Unfaithful, yet bewitched, a moment longer
Touching your chest, replying, then apart.

Dark – the scents it cannot repossess!
They hover, fretful, whispering, and haunt
With gratitude, regret, with fear, recalling
How love is want, how love is fear and want.

'And if I said so ...'

And if I said so, what would you reply?
If we swam out and never came back in,
Lapping against the deep end just the pulse
Of water, is it water? Just the kiss
Of waves against the tiles, if we swam out,
Or stepped out past the giant windows filled
Like pools with the reflections of our lives,
Onto the ragged grass, beyond the dog mess,
Into the trees and never came back out
But just the sound of birds that told them something
And just the silly pines that whisper, whisper,
As if to them, to say 'another absence',
Would they come after, or would they let us go,
And could we stay for ever, or a time,
Under the marbling wavelets, under the waving treetops,
And if for ever would we stay there truly,
Or if for a time would there at least be joy
And clarity, lips made for words, and lips
Made for saying things, and if I said so,
And if I said so, what would you reply?

'His father was a baker ...'

for A.G.G.

His father was a baker, he the youngest son.
I understand they beat him, and they loved him.

His father was a baker in Oaxaca:
I understand his bakery was the best

And his three sons and all his daughters helped
As children with the baking and the pigs.

I can imagine chickens in their patio,
At Christmastime a wattled turkey-cock, a dog

Weathered like a wash-board, yellow-eyed,
That no one stroked, but ate the scraps of bread

And yapped to earn his keep. I understand
The family prospered though the father drank

And now the second brother drinks, often
To excess. I understand as well that love

Came early, bladed, and then went away
And came again in other forms, some foreign,

And took him by the heart away from home.
His father was a baker in Oaxaca

And here I smell the loaves that rose in ovens
Throughout a childhood not yet quite complete

And smell the fragrance of his jet-black hair,
Taste his sweet dialect that is mine too,

Until I understand I am to be a baker,
Up before dawn with trays and trays of dough

To feed him this day, next day and for ever –
Or for a time – the honey-coloured loaves.

'After that night'

After that night,
After that night and this
The tight spirit was freed
To gaze down on its house
The way a bird might be
By a single rifle shot
Breaking the morning frost
At random and a man
In boots and tweeds crash through,
His cheeks aflame with cold
Or with another love.

And circling it saw –
That spirit of recoil –
The hours where it had lived
In the stout tree, its nest
A little sorrel fist,
Its chicks with open jaws,
The jackdaws in the brake
Eyes beaded out with lust;

And saw as well that man
Who held the gun with one
Still in the breach take aim
And look me in the eye
With such a searching love
The pellet could not miss.
The tight spirit was freed
To find where it would fall,
Sun winking on the steel
And in the lover's eye.

After that night and this,
The flash and then the fall,
After that night this day
With nothing left at all
Except the fist, the chicks,
The jackdaws in the brake,
Feathers on the lips
And lead beside a heart
That flutters and would fly
But cannot rise at all.

'I want to print them all'

I want to print them all,
each draft that led to this –
not the approximate poem
that rattles in its throat
but the drafts, the nights of slow
undressing that prepared
with give and take of pulse
this perfect nakedness.

This nakedness I'd name
and taste it on my lips
like Adam that first day
whom nothing could restrain:
his wild abundant tongue
had yet to learn deceit;
it was his paradise
he tied with words, and lost.

I write with my left hand
so that the right is free
to touch between the lines
the down upon your back
and weigh the quickened pulse
that fills you, and the soft
sack where you hoard your gift –
like Adam this first day –

but your mouth stops my words
before they tie you down;
you would suck out my heart,
the hammer in my chest
that drums each muscle tight
and skips in brow and wrist,
in the weapon and the wound
your rapid lips devise.

This perfect nakedness
we take and make in turn;
the words glow incandescent
that you won't let me speak –
they flare up as I turn

to take your nakedness.
I plant your gift. You gasp,
returning us to sound,

but sound so altered
we cling to it like fruit
twinned on one stem, we make
a final draft, an end
to stuttering nights, and fear
and solitude: it is
not sleep we find. But grace?

In paradise it's midnight
and nothing has been named.
A moon glows and some stars
kindle; then a breeze
shudders the leaves outside
so that the moonlight breaks
like liquid and like bread
on perfect nakedness.

The Love of Strangers

*'So, if one can keep oneself out of it, one may
present a picture of a sort of world and time.'*
Ford Madox Ford, *Return to Yesterday* (1931)

I

Easy to love the dead! So I love you more each year,
More tenderly, precisely draw you back
Into your landscapes – they ached without you ...
Your orchard of emerald domes and spires, of fruit
With pebbly skin, grown from the sticks you brought
Out of the clouds around Atlixco, Puebla.
Fuerte they called the tree
That stood against Pacific frosts
And learned to yield crates of fat fruit each season.
In that high village where you found the bud-wood,
Below the snow-line, New Spain's first poet
Endured her childhood: little bastard
In her grandfather's rustic library, somehow
Clutching a quill at his long table, 1660.
If I say I am fair, I say no more than is true;
Your eyes attest I am, my deeds prove me so.
Fair! That great medallion at her breast,
And shrouded (like your one daughter) in nun's habit!
A saint, severe from love and abstinence.
With her you shared thin air, dizzying vista –
Not century, language, faith. Severe you were,
From love as well, without theology, so that you died
In a night ward restrained by nameless sisters
And your ashes were salted over the rusty hectares
Of my godfather's poor ranch in Tamaulipas ...

I draw your little airplane edging along the Cuban coast
Like a moth enraptured by a sunlit velvet sleeve
Spread on an endless shelf of white-flecked blue.
You landed on an army polo field,
The horses crazed and rearing as you taxied,
The officers indignant, curious ...
Havana as it was, you the first human bird ever to land
In that promiscuous opulence. You'd flown across
From sober, parched Yucatan. Big headlines
Announced that Cuba was much less an island ...
Banquets, and the women. 'No papaya for me,' you said,
'I do not take to it.' Bursts of laughter behind fans,
Your host in a loud whisper, '*Fruta bomba!*
Here papaya has another meaning!'

Beyond gaping arches,
Steep cliffs of ficus, florifundio,
The shanties had another meaning, singing, Guillén's
Barefoot island ripened in its gullies, its sweet fields:
I'll drink you in a single gulp, dark girl, dark night;
Take off your robe of foam!
                    In my billfold
I have a photograph of you: 1919, Maracaibo Bay.
A pipe's clenched in your teeth.
You lean on the tiller of a little boat.
Who held the camera? *It's time you came back home,*
Your road is going wrong ... (Martí, the poet).
I recognize the rage stored in that frown,
Which burst, the way that fire destroys a cloud,
Chasing wild echoes round a hemisphere
And rain for days.
                    Then the California landscape,
A mortal splendour, you belong like the mountains,
The sea, far from the thickening centre, snared by no man.
My first memory's there: Capistrano,
The Big Acre, the avocado plantings,
Dragging old orange trees out with a fork truck,
Their short roots thick and squat like the roots of teeth.
Our reservoir, the rattlesnakes alarmed along furrows.
Gophers raised domes among the vegetables,
Pulling our well-grown asparagus
Stalk by stalk into their vaulted cellars. At night
Skunks with steaming broods crawled under the house;
We had to poke them out with sticks and shoot them.
We had a jeep and eucalyptus trees. How hot
All the days were, red grapes got ripe for the ants,
And the low house was haunted mornings, evenings,
By you, tall and dusty from your work.
                              That world ceased
When we moved back to Mexico, you sat down once more
At your big green roll-top desk and the heavy ledgers.
The truth is, you were continually outliving
Your fantasies – or you ran short of money.
Enchantments failed.
                    We were growing old. I was five.
At sixty your liberty had ended.
Sixteen years till your death – and the pain of losing
Year by year both memory and illusion. The boy

With the terrier who was such a superior ratter
In Torreon; in Aguascalientes, the massacre of the Chinese
When Villa was afraid to occupy the town
The Federals had deserted, leaving common folk
To their revenges, and your dad quickly
Boarded up the shop and hid as many Chinamen
As fit in cellars and attic; the Dictator
Three years earlier, omnipotent, relaxed,
Passing where you and your cousin Howard
In short trousers squatted fishing by the canal
At Xochimilco, and the old copper-faced *caudillo*
Smiled in the flowered barge, saluted you back ...
They got forgotten in the grim refrain
'I have about ten more years'; then the refrain
Got forgotten and you started coasting.

When you were a captain at the end of the First World War
– It's there you learned to talk like Teddy Roosevelt -
You went to France for the first and only time
To help assess the war debt. You saw Verdun
Where every inch of soil was overturned
And suddenly you were glad God hadn't answered
Your boy scout prayer for 'action'.
But when you're old things change;
An old man longs to have died young.
You would have done it well, and left behind
Hearts that only time and money mend.

And something remains apart from what you spoke of,
Something that's mine, I can't be sure of it.
                    Who showed me – it was you –
The great black rose window in some chapel –
And the Sequoiahs, did I go down on my knees?
And here below, a sad, a shadowy house ... and who is she?
I came – I must have come – full of love and my cot
Was cold, the room was cold. There were bears and creatures.
Days passed, you were the long hand of the clock
Morning and evening, morning and evening, time went by
With its feasts, its toys and solstices, till rose
And cold room were memory and less than that,
An almost deadened nerve; but the gilded cornices,
The steep sash, the sickles of the trees come back
Now that I have a son. How cold is his room?

I am standing tall myself
As a grandfather clock.
             If it were not for time
We could be brothers, the three of us.
As it is I feel your cheekbones in my smile,
Your gestures bend my arms and wag my head.
The pure tone of your whistle finds my lips
As if I was an echo, a reflection,
And you stood over there with your neutral smile
Watching what time, not silvered glass,
Does to the very last of your sloughed skins.
             Half of my life you've been dead
And yet not absent for a single day! I steer continually
By your prohibitions. 'Dear Papacito', school letters began
When most of the time I meant to wound. After all,
You'd sent me four thousand miles into exile
And called it education. I had grievances. I hurt you
Because you were too guileless not to trust me.
You wadded up draft after draft of your replies
But kept my letters in a drawer
In your steel roll-top desk at Pino 458.
After you died I found them stashed there
As if they were love letters. But this is the first.

II

If I'd known how well, after your death, I'd come to know you
That day you climbed four flights (and you almost eighty)
For an interview in Churton Place,
I would have taken more attentive note;
And the time we taped you down in Maiden Newton –
Late winter, pitch dark at five, thorned boughs across the door–
And caught your rusty voice doing 'Gloriana
Dying', with you dying ...
My heart wasn't in it.
             Now she's in deep:
You may imagine you're dead. I tell you different.
If dead, what are these spells you still weave? If dead
Why are you so indiscreet, your secrets spill
Like leaves from a frost-stung tree, with besom and basket
She gathers facts, as if such truth really mattered.
It puzzles me how you kept no secret from yourself,

You were your chronicler and stood in your own eyes
Naked as a girl half-loved, distrusted.
                    Wanting to write of you
I write of her. She climbs with her bright youth into your frame
And both of you are altered – merged? Married, is it?
She borrows your irony, or is borrowed by it;
Your styles were made for each other, but I love only her.
Just now she's away in your house, sleeps in your musty room
In the bed you died on, loved on, and she gives you
– You were a white witch – house room, heart room.
I say the rosary of her absence, doubt's *paternoster*
Meanwhile.
              You called me a rogue, your rogue cat liked me,
Sat on my lap, stitched me gently with his claws,
Needling, needling, hinting what he might do.
Was his name Tib, or Titus? Is he still alive,
Bleached by years, as you were: white witch, white cat ...
I say the rosary of her absence, she sleeps in your bed
Under coral rug, sea-blue counterpane, and moonlight sends
A foliage patchwork, webbing her face with summer,
Years of summer.
                    Jealous of the dead! No, afraid rather
Of her new intimacies. Oh, you had family,
They survive: cousins, eager of tongue, amiable,
Loving, loving.
                    Also a coven of friends
Strayed now through England. She makes her way
Like a nurse among them, nodding, smiling, noting symptoms,
Or like a good daughter in search of you
In the stale upper air where memories embroider the shroud.
Which is she, nurse or daughter? Daughter or wife?
The story of your life displaces hers, rebarbative,
And will not merge.
                    Release her back to me:
What sacrifice do I you require?
I cannot share with you: she is not Proserpine,
I am not Dis. She ate the fruit I offered whole, without remorse
Till latterly. I claimed her by contract where I named her –
Hardest of all to love, best loved of all.

III

One by one your friends
Fell to the force of sensible arrangements,
Sowed themselves in prosperous soil and grew
their various houses. In the high windows
Children's faces showed, and they came down.
We aged, our taproots deep in compromise
And money. We have become a benign forest now,
A little jealous of your delightful liberty.
We patronize you as we do the memory of our own youth,
As though you were a child
Who touched in us a silted innocence.

Free spirit! Free within this loving forest
Where you are home a few more easy years,
If there were a room here large enough
It would be yours for ever, as we are.
But can you settle with those words that are
Air and your air, and on that countryscape
Whose shapes conceal the lover that you seek?

IV

'He's in a home now,' Mr Stringer said, and with distaste,
'He shares a room with somebody.' He sank lower in his chair.
I sucked my drink and wondered:
                              what of his sons,
The impatient, youngish wife? He was impossible
And vain, but you got used to that. Perhaps his last marriage,
Apparently for love, had been a one-way street, he doting,
She comfortably killing time while years and illness
Made a meal of him.
                   Unkind, I chided myself.
                                  But did he merit
A final Home alone, coupled with a skeleton this time
Unchosen, and crippled so he could not crawl
Into a little limelight – go out at one of those soirees
With the comforting celebrity that friends provide
Who used to clap his poems and drink his wine?

'He'd got hard-up, I knew.'
Mr Stringer nodded. 'Got hard up.'

That he'd fallen all the way surprised me:
He'd been so prudent in earlier marriages,
As widower husbanding his shares, erect at his huge desk,
Lost in the contrived disorder of journals, books,
Paced by the local pulse of church bells, pen busy
With thin and thinner lines, then busy still with nothing.

'I last saw him when they changed his hip.'
'That's a good ten years back now.'
He lay in a private bed so frightened of pain, of dying,
That his eyes pleaded like a child's.

'In 1968 he welcomed me.
He dubbed me Facilitator.
I was to redress his quarter century's neglect.
I took him at his word, then had the task of letting go.'
'Oh, I knew him before the War, we sat it out together.
Both C.O. We're contemporaries, if anything,
I'm the elder.'

           What was the absence in his novels, poems?
Always a table for one, silver and crystal, the glow
Of pale candles, pale eyes focusing desire, but furtive,
Unable to name the heart, to lay a hand on the heart,
But in the mind's ferment, hard breasts, intelligent thighs.
Always a table for one, but large, with places laid
For those the mind invites, whose white unblemished flesh
Becomes momently real – then vanishes, not even a scent
Staining the intellect.
               'He always had a certain clarity.'
The clarity of platitude. 'But, poor chap,
He got his timing wrong.'
He abandoned his native Ulster – 'a black book
I never want to re-open'; but the Troubles made a fashion,
He took the volume down and dusted it. Too late for homing,
He left a page turned down just in case.
He aped Continental radicals, but gave them up
Years before their crossing from Dieppe.
He could always say (and did), 'I'm an Ulster poet'
Or 'I passed that way some time ago.' True,
But he never stayed.
            Chameleon! like Derain –
A quiverful of brushes, travelling each fashionable highway,

Altering his palette in ways that passed for genius
And sometimes was. This age is less generous. I've never known
A man so worldly, the right books on his shelves
If he could only lay his hands on them,
Cursory, eclectic, his optimism
Naive jetsam of a precocious childhood. By running on before,
Then running back with stale 'I told you so's',
A sort of prophet after the event, he passed as wise for a time.

In retrospect he must have drawn a hundred times the map
That leads to his blank bed, his faded page.
On principle he avoided the War but it took everything;
His history stopped at 1938 – *annus mirabilis*, the novel,
The great success that History swallowed.
                                    A man so eager
To catch the boat, and the boat pulling away, leaving him
With his trunk and hopes on the quay! He amazed me the first time
With his urbanity. Later he trotted out the same anecdotes
Like a soldier who chews your ear with one old battle.
Each time I went to his tall gilded flat he had
Something urgent to show me he just couldn't find
On those sagging shelves of literature, and evening
Folded us into dim armchairs, whiskies in our hands and him
Still talking, unwilling to let go.
                              The last time, too,
Reluctant to be seen, grimacing, tear-maps on his cheeks,
Then holding my hand in both of his and asking,
'How good am I? Tell me, how will my work be taken?'

                  Pain's grown like a tumor ...
Now he's a single knot of it or empty altogether.
I cannot visit him. He's too worldly to be seen
Shaved of vanities, naked on the quay for the little ferry boat
That this time comes to take him – is it to Ireland?

Mr Stringer rises. 'Time for dinner.'

Where I am as where he is the January air is cold,
Such lights as burn are not reflected by the lapping water.

V

If he'd been a bird he would have had no feathers:
Sharp beak, sharp talons, a voice pure as water
Just at freezing point, or the mind at sleep
On the point of transformation.
                    His last book's inscribed
Plein d'amitié – Janos Pilinsky; the first was fuller:
*Plein de remerciments et d'amitié: du sollst mich nicht
Vergessen.* That's how we talked in Babel, trading phrases,
The small change of language. Yet he meant it.

I tease out an image of yours: how she wipes the mirror,
For it strikes her that the frame is beautiful;
The glass should be worthy of it, of the room.
She polishes the dust away, the cobwebs,
Stands back and is rewarded by – herself.
Aproned, red-faced, her hairy arms and lip.
'At least the job is done.' 'At least it's true,
The thing she sees.' 'It's not the thing she sought.'
'She was not seeking, really. Was she seeking?'
'Not really, but like Picasso said, she found;
Like Saint Teresa, she found it in the stew,
In menial circumstance, in dailiness. She looked
And was dazed by the visual irony –
The gilt about *her*! The carved fruit and leaves
Framing the least servant, I forget her name.'
As if a murderer found he wore a halo
And was borne by an archangel at each hand.

You were borne by angels till they dropped you:
The army of heaven has become so clumsy.
You are dead now and I don't forget you,
Or how you startled yourself, incongruous
But real in the frame of every poem.
You were after gravity, and earth,
But found the rags of spirit on the wire,
And found the wire, too, and the flanking trench.

VI

He organized the crazy assault on Trotsky
In Coyoacán, he and an artists' gang,
But History had asked the victim out to dinner.
When Trotsky died, no artist held the spike.

He would happily have broken his neck to paint
A Sistine ceiling worthy of dear Stalin.
Not a single image of love! A better artist said
What we wanted we wanted without innocence.

Dead now – revolution's pimp, acrylic
Vandal, pornographer of ideology … Buried!
The ill-primed surface of skyscraper murals
Spills his genius in a steady drizzle of flakes.
I am an architect of clouds. Dustclouds.

Before his release from Lecumberi 30
I had myself driven each month to the prison,
Sat lovesick in my father's car and pined.
The chauffeur kept the engine ticking over.
In a sunlit cell at the front, where the big pirul tree
Brushed the tezontle with its plumes and seeds,
He was painting (I thought) in a light we shared.
He soured me against all I was made of,
All I would love.
                            When they released him in '68
I got myself invited to the opening at Misrachi's
Of his prison pictures. These images were new:
I'd never seen his surfaces up close,
His coarse, hacked lines, paint thicker than skin,
Seared, sold before the flaying was complete …
Faces boiled, each finger broken – butcher more than painter:
If he'd been given our actual bodies, with his palette-knife
What would he have made of my father and me?
The organ of our syndicate, he wrote, was *El Machete.*
He dreamed of leading *organized masses.*
His pictures sold to American collectors.
                                          And here he was,
Out of his cage, short, shaggy, scented with Right Guard,
Lean-faced but the body stout with long confinement.
He autographed catalogues with a Pepsi biro.

I waited in a queue, watching for the man
Who had led the revolution of the image,
Commanded Orozco and Rivera, erased the names
Of *individual painters* as too bourgeois.
When my turn came he wrote
David Alfaro Siqueiros
In inch-high characters.

Orozco, while a boy, was maimed in an explosion.
He lost a hand, his eyes were damaged. Out of pride
He had to be an artist anyway, out of love and pain.
Rivera learned to paint because of women, stones and mirrors.
Again it was Leda and Lethe. It was Narcissus.
Both men outgrew Siqueiros. Artists don't want leaders.
Revolution, Orozco said, *paints no pictures.*
He left the syndicate with half a dozen others.
We all fell out with Siqueiros.
                        Why can't I put out of mind
Those coiling gourds of his last prison period,
Those gourds that twist on their rough dish
And rise, as if they grew
From that captivity into the world
His revolution has not made?
And there were zinnias, white fire, walls
Falling, rifles, bones; he grew
Into himself in prison, like Genet,
Holding a brush in one hand and his hard
Penis in the other, not for love:
Art of a damaged son, child of a damaged land
Pygmalion, making a thing he must control,
Praying History to put colour in its cheeks.
When it steps free of the easel will it speak
From his own lips? Muddying his palette
With rage and desperation, his changing heart
Was never in this world.
                        Architect of clouds.

VII

I knew a tired old man in Islington.
'History skirted me, we never actually met.
Not really. Not in France, and not in Spain.
I was too clever for it: look at me.

I've lived this far.' By that, he seemed to mean
Too long, the way survivors do who clutch
Tight to life, in terror and resentment.

History grazed him, anyway. He lost
All his friends and one eye in the trenches;
Then a wife back home. Spain harvested
A second generation. Madrid he could remember, '37 –
Steep ruins, corpses, and the writers' prattle.

He surrendered to the Party, mind and pen,
As an acolyte embraces a dark priesthood
Out of a hunger for the crucified,
The passion of a man whose single pain
Longs for the facelessness of commonwealth.
He burned his future while his foes burned books.
They burned men, too; but so did his comrades. Winter
Frothed like grave alyssum on the wound.
The hole was never filled in: was a mouth
Bearded with foliage, without a tongue,
Receiving every year new generations,
Green tribes, raw heresies that tasted sweet.
Who ever heard of graves with such a hunger?
It was all a mad idea, except the hunger.

In 1956 he drew the line. Until then
The idea usurped his skull, translating
Justice, love, into its idiom.
Even when he broke faith it held him:
He repeated parrot-fashion stupid things
He must have known untrue, he had no energy
To start again, there was no place to get back to,
Nowhere, even though he was the first
English pilgrim to Rimbaud, he raised Donne from the grave
And brushed him down, and said 'Remember Swift,
He's neither dead nor sleeping – we are.'

When I first met him, at a little dinner party,
He was inaudible, stared at his hands.
He almost could not see them even then,
Fumbled with them, as if memorizing.
Three years later he took shape for me,
Obliging, as a tree will fill with leaves.

I shaded there trustingly, we talked,
Teasing memory, drinking his vodka.
'I can remember much forgetfulness,
As Hart Crane said if I remember rightly ...
I printed some of his poems, and once I met him
In London, did I tell you?' He had told me,
And written 'Poets' Fare'. I said he hadn't.

One weekend in his native Essex
We went to the coast. Blind then,
He pointed back the way we'd come and said:
'Out there you'll see the groin, and then
The bigger water.' Gently I adjusted
My friend, like a compass needle, towards the shore.
He clutched his stick. I took his arm,
This old man six years younger than my father,
And like my father wounded, like him blind.

Who was he? Now he's dead he comes
Sharply into focus, yet I cannot
Interpret him, not simple saint or fool.
What I knew was an old man in Islington
Who gave me everything he had in mind;
Who loved his language first, the tongue
Of Donne and Swift, and loved it last as well,
However many detours he took home
Along the English road, out of a fastness
That never understood him. His England
Had its own radicals, with their honed passions
Speaking plainly to plain-hearing men.
They were what he was made of, he became
One of their brotherhood, and shares their hearth.

VIII

Even a brief visit cannot exclude her,
My dark mother, who confused my blood.
How old she is now! Like the shawled Indians
Who used to mumble rosaries when she sneaked me
To church without my parents' knowing.
She said the Latin spells over and over.
What did they mean? I knelt at her elbow,

My eyes took in a hunched scrum of old women,
With soles calloused and chapped like baked soil.

The editor handed back my review:
Why write peasant Spanish,
A man like you, with your education?
Send it to me in English. I'll get it translated
By someone who sins less against the language.

If I could introduce him to my teacher!
I have only her to blame,
Her and her village – Cuacalco, under the squat hill.
One time she took me to see where she grew up –
Without a father, I later deduced; where she bore
Her one child without a husband, left him
To an aunt when my father gave her work.
And how she worked! Dark mother, dark grandmother,
Fed me, kept me clean, let me ride on her back,
Taught me her language, told me her story
Time after time, always the same words,
Yet the same words real as though she'd just found them.
I was the stand-in for her dismal baby,
She called me *hijo;* last time I visited
She took for granted I was her only son.

She's not poor now. At market
They call her Doña, step aside to let her pass
But behind her back say *hechicera*, witch,
Her herbs and charms are famous. She gets
Chickens, coins, tin amulets for her intercessions,
She cures the neighbourhood. Her saints

Hear her without fail. She has her faith
As other folk have air to breathe, yet asks
Nothing for herself. She cannot read or count.
She has forgotten nothing in eighty years.

I know the powdery fields she worked as a girl, the *jacales*
Wearing tin or tile roofs slanted to black
Doorless openings, the irregular pulse
Of animal and human habitation, smoke rising
Straight on breezeless days like stems of gold,
At mountain-height dilating in blue.

The church, begun in 1612, never completed, barks
Its two bells, the women kneel,
Drunk with labour, prayer and the scent
Of arum lilies, incense, stale wax, flesh.
Their children hang on them like fruit.
Bead-eyed madonnas and their Christs survey
The ragged flock franchised by the beatitudes.

There was, she said, a snake – and claimed she'd seen it –
They call it pasture-snake there in her *tierra*.
It lives on milk. When it finds cows grazing
It writhes up a leg and fastens to an udder,
Drawing until the cow is dry.
When a nursing mother falls asleep,
The snake comes, fastens to the breast,
Giving the child its tail for pacifier.
If it comes just once, the child won't live.

Even the briefest visit home cannot exclude her,
Though now she always cries when I see her and needs
More love than I have, so I give her money.
Some debts, when language fails, have to be settled crudely –
When love and language fail.

IX

The long blind wall towards Oxford pebble-dashed,
Moss-blotched, veined with ivy; a gravel drive
Unraked, visited by nurses and by me
Who leaned my bicycle against a trellis,
Rang at the blank door.
                    You left the chain on,
Sprung the latch, with a 'Yes?' like a hinge being forced,
Always in dark glasses, glamorous, faded.
'When I first met you,' I said on my third visit,
'I thought you were your daughter.'
'We chose not to have children,' you said,
'And kept our youth for a time. Now we're old.'
He slept on a bed in the living room (could hardly move –
You'd abandoned the top storey years before).
Blind to the north, to the south the house
Took in with its wide windows all of Berkshire.
He lay stone-deaf, like the battered river-god you'd find

72

At an ancient spring, gazing on treetops, cloudscapes,
At night the *embers of the living towns*.

From such a height it hardly looked like England,
Scored by the calligraphy of ancient roads
And tiled with variegated fields that seemed the bed
Of a broad pool peculiar to one palace. 'Just before
We came home from Persia, father had it built.
It's cleverly done.'
                    Heat swam
Like water over the Berkshire plain.
You were already blind except to misprints, certain flowers.
Concise, precise, civil, unsentimental, abstract words
Throng to describe you, like so many doves
Loosed from neglect to a hand that scatters bread.
They seek you not because you were over eighty
And abstractions love old age and the dead,
But since you brought to bear on your tradition
Purities of logic, Persian, mathematics,
Tools that served you, as you thought, supremely.
I typed and re-typed your last essay, 'The Roots
Of Unity', from large-scale handwriting on lined sheets
Like a child's crude exercise –
Phrases and formulae like the root system
Of a plant grown wise and beautiful, and frail
So it sends thin fingers out to hold.
                              Perhaps they hold,
I cannot understand them, though I know for you
Logic was a passion, commanding fever as the flesh will do,
Or as those windows took command of Berkshire.

'We had a proper garden.' How unlike English pastoral
Your acres must have been, though starred and stained
With familiar blooms. Even now the banks and rusty lawns
Make sense in terms of everything around them,
Interpreting, not distorting, their context.
If, when I entered your cool, dazzling rooms
I seemed to step out of the present tense,
It was only history I wiped off my shoes on the mat
To enter stable time: season, solstice, fruit,
As Horace did, leaving Rome for his Sabine farm,
Cooling his wrists in a spring unfenced, unfouled.
'We get up with the sun. Most of the winter we sleep.'

Aloof from the *blind nurses of racial character*
You evolved a mystic disregard for commerce,
For war, assassination; instead adhered
To what does not change, is not destroyed,
What you share with Sumer, Greece and Alexandria,
With Amherst, Weimar. Hampton Court,
Curious territory no single map contains,
A *Geist* without race, which cannot be annexed,
Enjoined, perverted, a refinement
Hungry for forms and the few sharp timeless truths.

The *barren severities* of history, Persia taught you,
Made no lasting wound on a real culture,
Any more than the adjustments of an intellectual border
Affected the capital of human sense –
As if Darwin, Marx and Freud had not clouded the sky
With their unsettling breath; how long have they lived
Compared with Homer? What is their style,
Have they really touched language or only words?
Would this plane, this beech
This cypress tree survive in Eden or Utopia,
Or only here?
                    The mind is a garden, as the garden is,
And hangs above a wilderness it comprehends.
To lose sight, to see the garden fade out gradually,
Not because it changes, but we change,
Brings round the last term of old wisdom, death,
Clean of fear and superstition.
The tiny islands of pleasure, the reefs where love ran aground
Are lost, each private temple falls, and yet,
As you knew they would, the week you died
The flowers kept their scent,
And not a word you wrote became less true.

X

I don't keep up with your wives, the sisters:
How are they? One dead? Both dead? Your broken daughter,
Does she still wander around her locked and loving hostel
Looking for you, or a tree, or any sharp thing?
That night at your house she stared at me and stared
And you said how when she was three the eczema
Had eaten off her innocence; you clutched her

74

Night after night like a starfish to your chest
So she would not chew herself, so she would not bleed.
And you kept her as long as you could, she grew to a girl,
To a young woman with dark, unsettled eyes
Who played with gas- and water-taps; once, naked,
Got out into the street, wandered down the hill
Curious about the way her skin changed colour
When she walked under the trees, and in shade changed texture
As gooseflesh came in the chill and subsided in sunlight.

The night I came to your house, the power cuts –
It was the three-day week – returned the hill to Keats's century.
No cars, no jaundiced street-lamps, only
Candle-light through curtains; gaslight, firelight.
When I knocked you answered the door holding a candle
In one of those brass dishes with an ear and lip.
By candlelight you let me see your pictures –
Bottles, most of them, not like Morandi's
But made of light and oil, of breasts, of skin.
Faint, ghostly – how they haunt me; some critics called them,
When they showed them at the Tate to mark your death –
Called even the late ones, even the ones where red
Bursts in like fire, or rage – 'serene' and 'cold',
As though the distance from the canvas
Imposed by brush, by fingers, and the hours
You spent before them cooled the focused passions
That punished your gentle body, your handsome face
In those fast weeks, as the cancer ate you,
Even that time, two months before your death.

While we talked you kneaded little lumps of wax
Between your restless finger-tips, then lost them.
'And my poems,' you said, patting a pile of them.
'I've spent the last twelve months getting them into order.
They're numbered, and the sequence matters –
At least,' you added, like a boy, glanced shyly
Out of the dark window at the dark, 'at least
I believe it matters, there is an argument.'
The poems – 'They will not sell.' They have not sold.

Where did they come from? Who chose the bottles?
What caused the uncompromised heart of this dead man?
First the huge silence, then love and its implements –

Palette, knife, tubes, blank canvas like stillest water
Of a lagoon waiting a shaping breath;
And on the table, cool surfaces of glass.
How could you exclude
Memory, or love, or the broken child?
Your paintings move from grace and natural hunger
To pain, and death too has its palette.
Those sleepless nights you fought with your fallen angel
And lost have marked you. You remain awake
For ever, like a figure out of Dante.

It's winter; the lights will not come on
In that stark memory. I walk down the hill.
He is dying. I carry in my satchel
His poems, his and Piper's Venice,
And in a red card binding
'The Impact of Architecture': *if we speak*
On occasion of an eye-window, it is not
To suggest that it sees but that a break
In the wall is like a socket. Buildings
Are images of blindness ... At midnight
The lights came on, I had walked half way home.
I read his essay on the tube and he was dying
Even as I puzzled at it. His city was dying,
The hill was burning, glowing like a coal,
Flaring and cooling towards the morning, and I
Was twenty-four. Urbino I had not seen. Rapallo
I have not seen. I've read now – watching his mouth,
Watching his dancing hands – his Rimini, his Florence.

We are waiting for Ruskin, for Pater, your natural family.
When they home from their travels you'll emerge
At your white door with its Georgian fanlight,
But then in broad daylight. 'Where have you been?' you'll say.
Waiting for the right time, which is now, you're at last
Released from the hostel of neglect; your mother is gone
And your daughter, your wives, the world of women.
Here are your canvases, the bottles replenished
With claret and white light, with amber, green.
The world that made you has at last gone down;
You are released to this unmaking world
By your pliant lucidity and those
Discreet charged images that flare.
'They will not sell.' Not yet, they will not sell.

XI

Is there a limit to how many changes
A man can go through between his first love
And the one that bursts his heart?
And with those changes, a kaleidoscope of views –
From cellars and high balconies, sober and drunk –
Always the same city flanked by the same hills,
Washed by a sea as filthy as the shore.
But the rough boys grew suave; cheap fashions bought them,
Poor mutants of affluence and bigotry.

Each year, it seems to me, you altered colour –
Not as the chameleon to hide
But to be vivid like an ulcer or a bloom.
I follow after and – two decades late –
Look for your footprints in the shantytowns.
Here are the children of the child you loved
In endless transformations as he was,
And I see what dragged you in and out of guilt
Like a fish on a sharp hook but a weak line:
You boarded the midnight tram to what you wanted
Regardless of the price – which was your life.

I met you once at a reception in London
Held in a low-ceilinged room by the river
With writers you despised. You approached me
And said, 'How very English of you: an umbrella,
On such a night as this!' In your smile
I counted the teeth. I'd come down from Oxford
Not to hear you but Auden.
I'd not even seen your films, much less read
A word of yours in verse or prose.
You had a haggard look, also a hunger
To be out of there, back in your element.
I didn't understand your manner. 'Goodnight.'
I hurried off to Paddington for the train.

I wish I'd lingered at least a few minutes
In your solitude that evening in London,
Simply to learn your voice, to taste
The ashes of Casarsa from your lips. What errors,
What pain it might have helped me round, to hear

Just for a moment in that crowded room
The pure elixir of your egotism,
The Italy that coarsened your tongue with love.

XII

Greek, Latin and Italian were required
For Comp. Lit. 201. I had Latin
And elementary perjury. They got me
(Like some others) into the dark
Upholstered room.
He sat, drowsy, possessed,
Not at the table head but at the long side,
Like Christ among disciples, mainly girls.
In our different hearts we worshipped him;
He smelled as sweet to us
As Alexander on the field of battle,
His heavy-lidded eyes steady as a falcon's.

We addressed – or he did – Narrative,
The epic observed by lyric eyes
('The only eyes we have these days').
The course that should have sped from Homer down
Through Virgil to Dante, Milton, Perse
(Whose *Birds* he rendered, with Braque's lithographs)
Stalled somewhere in *Odyssey* Book IV.

'Forget the *genre*, epic's not Homer's word –
And anyway, who was he?' We read Lord
And Parry, learned to doubt, while he recited.
'Forget the page, hear the words in air.'
He hung them there like notes
From staves of silence our attention made.
'We ought to shut all but the book of memory,
But leave that open like an ear.'
                    The Muse was real
To Homer and to him, Penelope not a trope
But a weaver whose desire
Plucked notes from the loom, and a lover back
From deep water, deep time, even out of death's
Cavern, where Virgil followed, and then Dante.
There he now squats on the hollow hill
Instructing them.

In the course of other adventures,
In another country, I am reminded of you
By your death. Haven't I thought of you before
In twenty years?
                    Once, maybe,
On the spoiled site of Ilium
Where I could have gathered sacks of clam-shells.
I reflected on the diet of Homer's tedious characters
And sensed how far I was from your Homer's world.
Your death now simply tells me I've forgotten
The word is sacred. I've grown out of it
Into the secular.
                    Once you assessed
Some poems. I gave you forty. 'I read the first
And thought there's really something here.
It wasn't there in the other thirty-nine.'
Did I thank you? Now I thank you: elegy,
Imagined reparation.
                    In memory you're not dead
But away on your blue island, practising
A hundred voices against the inattentive tide.
In the *Odyssey* Zeus speaks early on, 'The poem's
Airborne almost at once'; for many, you were the first
To make the sequence of words we call a poem
Audible; you moved us more than an instrument,
Zeus of our adolescence, maker, mover,
Yet I remember not one line of yours.

It is winter, my idols have all shed their leaves.
There is no fruit, no shade, a weight of snow
And, caused by death to think of you, a weight
Of sadness that falls short of grief.

Here are some faded notes from my spiral book.
The page headed 'Homer, Virgil, Dante'
And underneath, 'hero, patriot, priest'.
'Battle was made for poets; if they were true,
Words blinded them until they saw with words,
Leaving the sharpened vision of poems.'
'Poets, like Iopas, may live to have white hair,
Harps of gold, and kings to listen
While taking loving census of their slaves.'

I'm sure you never said such stuff, it was me
Sententiously mishearing, I always did. I do.
Yet without malice, played on by your voice.
Auden says the poem reads us. You might have said
The poem makes us worth reading.
Love is somewhere near the poet, jealous,
Seated beside him, beside you, across the table, in dark
Recesses, folded tight on its deception,
Hungry in devotion, watching, writing,
Its corpse quite bare beneath its ignorant toga.

XIII

I opened my porthole the first morning
Intending to say *ma'haba* to the Nile
And a yellow mouse jumped into my sleeping sheet.
I checked out of the youth hostel barge
And into a hotel on 26 July Street.

Waiting for you I had two days to kill.
My map was all in French. After an hour at the wrong
Bus stop, I was appropriated by Farid Fahmy,
A teacher keen to try his English. He talked me up
The Citadel, the Sultan's sequinned mosque,
Ibn Tulun, El Mu'ayyad, El Azhar,
The medersa, the suqs; at last we came
To rue El Hassan and climbed to his flat
High on a cliff of habitations,
A crumbling summit where we sat in shadow.
There were no doors on his storey. It was held in common.
We ate orange quarters cooled in water,
Served in a blue bowl by a palsied aunt.
On the balcony his kid brother took my elbow
And pointed out the sights. I met his doves.
The boy lifted one out of its rustic cote
Gently, as if handling a flower,
Then hurled it at the sky.
Other doves followed in an arc of white
Pure against khaki sand, grey concrete, yellow sky,
Blown upwards, solid flakes of brilliance offered
To the god of hospitality.

You and I
Met as planned at Giza, under the trite Sphinx's gaze,
By her right paw. At the Sphinx cafe in town
(It was soon after the Six Day War, the buildings
Were sand-bagged, Israeli jets flew low
Breaking the sound barrier twice a day)
We wondered how we might join *El Fatah*.
I confess I committed murder in my heart
And so did you, we were so hot with virtue,
Remote from the actual sources of our rage.

You get used to talk, to traffic, heat,
The amazing daily ritual of the wealthy
At Groppi's, shovelling icecream into their boredom.

Each time we stopped on our way up the Nile
We got arrested. As luck would have it,
Your Lebanese Arabic was suspect. One night
The officers came back for us in a black Mercedes,
Drove us at top speed into the dark,
Braked hard above a scroll of fluid moonlight,
Switched off the ignition and we heard
The unearthly belching chorus of Nile frogs.
The sergeant explained: sometimes his men got bored –
They thought we'd like to hear the serenade.

At Tel-el-Amarna we both fell in love
With a willowy serving-girl whose eyes
Kept meeting ours. You spoke a line of poetry to her
And found she was some sort of boy ... In the train
(Third-class, half-fare for students)
We were offered hard-boiled pigeon-eggs
And sung to, touched, our foreignness and pallor
A talisman. We slept as they did
On luggage racks ... One place
We crossed the river in a brown felucca
Like a dragonfly blown slowly over sunlight
And found the tombs we'd come for
Defaced with bright official slogans about the future.
Returning, we were pursued by a gang of kids who chanted
Israeli, Israeli, and levelled stones at our heads.
I have a scar, the only wound from my engagements there.

By donkey into the Valley of Kings, past the stumps
Of Ozymandias' legs; in Karnak
High on a wall of the holy of holies the word
Rimbaud cut deep in stone; by the Pool of Frogs
And a huge pink granite scarab among papyruses
We took mint tea and a shisha, served by another androgyne ...
The moon came up red, floating out of the palms
Huge as Achilles' shield, in the sky, in the pool,
Praised by ecstatic frogs, climbed clear of the tallest
Column, the last lotus capital, and began to cool.
We watched it go to coin size, turn white,
Silver white; we sipped mint tea,
Scalding our hearts, then scalding them again.

XIV

You taught me chess when I was six,
Just so you'd have someone to beat
In a leisurely way, not so I'd take much notice.
You advanced white pawns and knights until at evening
My queen fell to your bishop, my king resigned.
Formally you shook hands, muttered a German phrase.
We climbed to supper. A servant cleared the board.

When you were twelve and broke your leg
Your father beat you first for carelessness
Then summoned the physician. Prussia
Claimed your little homeland five years later.
The Emperor came right past your front door
Requiring homage, riding rather badly
On a huge horse proportioned for a statue.

You fled the Imperial Recruiting Officer,
The wars he had in mind not wars you'd choose.
Once on the road, you fled for decades.
My favourite failure! Like me a youngest son,
Deserter, optimist; dear, reluctant modern man, uprooted
From the tall family house by Pauleskirche
With office and stores at street level, and above,
The family rooms, almost prosperous,
Silent with formal tensions, sleeves and collars
Getting frayed but rigid with starch
And grey as dough. Uprooted

From the narrow garden
That plunged to the brisk, unfriendly river ...

You fled west with the human flood of disaffection,
Settled in Kansas, then Colorado, down the map
To Mexico, then south, then further south ...
Dogged still by history – Prussia, Pancho Villa,
Liquidators, conscience: almost prosperous
Time after time, shopkeeper, impresario, clerk;
Almost destitute.
                Failure's hero, you could not acknowledge
The huge vindictive goddess riding her storm cloud
Behind your little billowing wake of dust
Down the spine of both Americas
Until your final venture failed in Chile.

Five decades of declining years
Under the kind, unjudging care of my aunts,
And the President of the United States himself,
The Irish one, *und auch Papistisch*,
Wished you a happy century.
And even that was not the end of it
At Mar Vista, your dogs, hours on the porch just swinging
On the plaid garden seat. I was presented to
Old ladies you were allowed to court.
There was your case of rusty books, the regimented
Gothic tombstones of your complete, uncut Goethe,
And you subsiding into German.

You so enjoyed chess with me! I've forgotten the rules
But keep the tone in mind of your guttural
Crowing when you won. It pleased me to surrender
My little Saxon king with his pellet of lead ballast
That kept him upright in the evening breeze. I've fled as far
East as you fled west. Conscription, history, accident
And the vindictive goddess riding home
Mistook me for you.
                You'd recognize this house
If you came to the door tonight. You'd like to stay.
I have your chessmen in a box on the piano.
You'd know just where I've been, where I am bound to,
But being as you are, you'd spread the board.
We'd play in silence and you'd not let on.

XV

It wasn't snowing but it should have been.
You were an old man, nine months from the grave.
Your hand was very dry and very hot
And large, as I recall (I was a boy,
Fourteen years at most, I led you round
Part of the school, your guide; you seemed to listen).
That night you read in a slow, dismissive voice
That left the words like notes on staves hung in the air,
No longer yours, but part of memory –
You talked about Miss Dickinson of Amherst
And said aloud the eight lines of her poem
'The heart asks pleasure first'. And from that night
I've known the poem word-perfect, part of me.

I think you let more lines free into language
And memory with your rusty, lonely voice
Than any other poet of our age.
It must have been like freeing doves
And watching them go off to neighbouring cotes
Or into the low clouds of your New Hampshire
Knowing they'll meet no harm, that they'll survive
Long after the hand that freed them has decayed.

Those lines are wise in rhythm and they lead
Into a clapboard dwelling, or a field,
Or lives that prey upon the land and one another,
Or the big country where we both were children.

XVI

Idols, icons, dust; those hideous
Counter-Reformation Jesuses
Whose brows are purple thorn-cushions, hands pierced
As if candle-wax had oozed
Thickening from the wounds, the feet, the side;
Fingers too fine to be a carpenter's ...

Yours weren't: your impatient little hands indifferently
Healed wood or clay, as a doctor's might.
You taught yourself. 'I had to start somewhere,
So I did forgeries. Quite good ones, too.'

You styled yourself 'artist'. A restorer
Is artist, I suppose, in the sense a skilled
Editor once in his life's a poet, when he reads
Through ten corruptions a first clarity.

I left your stale apartment always sneezing
As if I'd been in a mine. I blew my nose
And made clay-coloured stains on the white linen.

Your two rooms held two families: in the first
Seven children coted in bunk beds
And your own double bed like an unkempt mainland,
Heart of that stifling archipelago;
Your wife with young amusing eyes and a body
That hung on her heavily, like dough,
And kept surprising you with births, miscarriages
And illness – she brought us tea
In gilded cups from her black scullery ...
And then the second room: the coffin-sized radio-victrola
With its sea-green hearth-light, an L of seats,
Your books in heaps on which the dust
Established colonies and spread on spider highways
Up to the ceiling with its dim fruit of light;
And the shelves, the boxes where the saints and Christs
– Most of them in transit – gloomily
Waited your touch, when their wings or haloes
Were readjusted, or the cross affixed
To shoulder or heart again, the eyes
Renewed with beads like tiny marbles,
To be sold, or sent back to their churches ...
They didn't interest me. I came to you
For idols, talk of idols, talk of ruins;
You knew them all, each Pre-Columbian site,
And though you liked them less than the saints and angels,
They were your livelihood as trafficker, restorer.
They had no temples to return to now.
History betrayed them into *objets d'art*.

I like to think my weekly visits
Renewed your pagan interests: when you played
A few notes on a Mixtec ocarina
Your poor, unsanctified rooms became a shrine.

At your suggestion we finally travelled
South and east, to see, never to buy.

You cradled those terracotta corpses,
Some brightly painted and some
Grey-brown like your own tired skin,
Gingerly, with superstition, with resentment, too,
That they remained strange and would not come clear.
You were willing to sell them to a young collector
But felt, as well, for all your generous knowledge –
More than a scholar's, knowledge of the palm
And finger-tip, the nose, the tongue –
Each sale an infidelity to them:
Not that you did not know their value;
You did not know their meaning, and that hurt you.
'What god is this? From the beaked mouth
It might suggest Ehecatl, the wind;
And yet the stylized foot belongs to the war-god.
Why then does he carry maize and a rattle,
What are those holes in his brow?'
'Are you sure you married up the proper fragments
Or is this a new god, drawn from several idols?'
I took it home, catalogued it 'Veracruz' –
The province you came from, and your sons all have
Totonac features; I had statuettes
From the thirteenth century they might have modelled for.
Your history has been plundered of its facts
Yet its blood flows, without memory, sometimes pure.

It must be strange to start from ignorance
And gather fragments of a shattered world,
Paste them together, add missing ears and arms,
Then sell them, strangers you have come to know
Intimately, but without a name.

You took me once to Merida. We spent
Days at the Mayan ruins and in churches.
One afternoon we visited a brothel (at thirteen
I did not know a brothel from a café).
You liked a big girl and went with her.
When you'd been gone ten minutes I got worried,
Followed down the dull-lit corridor
To where, at the end, over a half-door like a bar-door,

I saw you mounted on her like a locust
Perched feeding on a bloated aubergine.
I was suspended between nausea and laughter
To see you there so earnestly at work
Fitting yourself to that tumescent body,
Restorer! you were in your middle fifties
Under the little neon cabinet
In which an icon stared out like a fish
Into the distance of its own reflection.
That evening we went to Kabah: palaces
Of Tlaloc with the rain-god's stylized beaks
Hung like quotation-marks in stone, suggesting
'Temple', 'Hallway', 'Sacrifice'. 'You need
A guide?' 'Not us, no thanks,' you said, and yet
The Mayan boy took me by the elbow
And guided me to what he called the 'catacomb'.
Then rain, out of the blue, it seemed, unseasonal,
Confined us in a corbelled passageway
Startled by lightning, and the boy's face close,
His hand firm on my arm, him whispering
Words in his language, I supposed, while you called to me,
Thinking you'd lost me, and I couldn't answer –
Speluncam Dido dux et Troianus eandem
Deveniunt, as if Virgil had dumped me there.

The rain stopped, the boy released me.
My pulse was altered, we walked arm in arm –
His profile was off the friezes at Palenque,
His language had survived an ended culture –
Until we found you sketching in evening light.
We walked towards the highway and the dark
Began to smoke down on us; then the fireflies,
Erratic as my pulse, turned ground to heaven
With their rushing green-and-silver starlight.
Nobody had anything to say.
We hitched a ride back, left the boy half way.

I saw your workshop sign on Insurgentes
Last time I was home, and through your window
Your son José at work with tools. On what?
I should have called.
Odd how much of one is inadvertently
Borrowed, not acknowledged or returned.

I should have asked for news of both of us,
Rung at your dark apartment for strong tea
In a gilded cup, the gramophone; and, yes,
On the steep common balcony, your wife's
Green parakeets in their shrill tenements.

XVII

Being twelve was something, after all:
'Four o'clock,' he wrote, 'the twenty-fifth.
Calle del Buen Tono 347.
Punctually.' The writing feathered, frayed,
The hand of an old man, brisk but trembling.
'I cannot teach you Nahuatl, but if
You're half as dedicated as you suggest
I can advise. Bear this in mind, however:
No language is given apart from the one
The infant sucks in with a mother's milk.'
As though that mattered! He had written back!
I felt as if the good Lord had consented
To a brief audience with his altar-boy.

I lifted his books down in armfuls from my shelves.
I'd been collecting them for two years – thirty volumes.
Which would I ask him to inscribe? I cut the pages
And bent the spines of each so he'd know I'd read them.

It was the fourteenth when his note came.
I had eleven days, hardly time to change
Into the boy who'd posted that 'dedicated' letter.
I started turning page after page of his scholarship,
Soon yawned, stared at all I had to do and did not do it,
Imagining instead how he would be
As if his disciplines would have spared an actual man!
Could I become his apprentice and absorb
What he knew of Aztec, Otomí,
Of the little languages, and Greek and Latin,
Hebrew, Persian, Sanskrit? ('We cannot
Value our own or know how tall we stand
Without knowing the world.') One critic wrote,
'He was old even before Babel and for fun
Devised the tongues that divide men,
Exchanging them with God for the gift of years.'

My father's chauffeur drove me down through suburbs
So drab I shut my eyes. As we drew near
The Calle del Buen Tono, children pointed,
Indicating which way we should go.
The only unfamiliar traffic in these streets
Came hunting out their old priest, Father Angel.

I arrived 'punctually'. He was still out –
On his rounds among the hungry and illiterate, I supposed.
Yet his books were there, crowding every wall.
Two very small old women, swaddled in shawls,
Distrustful, fretful, supervised my waiting
Where I sat on a low hard chair, beginning
To see how much he'd written that I'd missed,
How much I'd missed in any case.
Through three rooms (the doors wouldn't close for books)
A solid library of his tongues.

He translated Greek badly, Latin badly;
The Aztec he rendered as though
The nineteenth century had dawned yesterday
In all its brutal freshness on the heart.
But he knew the Aztec language perfectly from books
Having transcribed the chronicles, annotated
The sacred hymns, the prayers, the chants of war;
He was Sahagún and every lesser witness,
Ghosting the figures buried in the silt
Of histories that History had displaced.

I'd not imagined rooms
So dusty, cold, so inhospitable,
Rooms like a dictionary, without waste
Or scruple, good manners or good cheer.
Then he appeared before me and I rose
Too quickly for politeness, more like fear.
His arms hugged his chest, as if he was cold in a shroud,
His hands and face were bleached, his beard, his eyes too seemed
All whites. I never saw a creature so bloodless,
As though he had strayed out of the past,
Or a cloud, or a grave. 'Don Angel!' I exclaimed,
Unfolded his reluctant hand
And did what the Indians do, I kissed it.
And then I blushed because I wasn't Roman Catholic

Or Christian. For the first time in my life
I smelled on him the stale scent
Of utter solitude and abstinence,
Of a man without vanity of the flesh,
Of Jerome, the smell of the desert,
The lonely scholar and the chaste shepherd.
What were his angels? Angels without wings,
The lame and halt, the kind whose place in heaven
Is guaranteed by the beatitudes.

One of the women brought sour coffee on a tray.
We had little to say. He found me out
With two or three sharp questions.
He was not angry that he'd wasted time
On such a green hypocrisy; there was
Only illusion, not malice, in my visit.
I had no discipline, no faith, and that was clear,
Nothing but a boy's ephemeral charm; to him
There was no music but philology, not sun
But candle-light.
                    I stood in the poor street
Outside the scholar's house. Father Angel
Did not see me off; I'd said goodbye
And he turned on a swivel chair back to his work,
Transcribing manuscripts so old,
Each time he turned a page they dwindled further
Towards that extinction which he chronicled.

I felt how distant my home was from his,
And being twelve was not so very much.
I left behind that day, in a heartless house,
One future I was sure I wanted.
Still on my shelves I have his books, and now
I've read them, and he's dead; yet he does appear
Out of the English snow, out of stale study air
From time to time, not to haunt, but qualify
My seriousness, to say, 'You are not a boy any longer.'
He is pale and bloodless with the purity of exile –
The exile of the dead from pure vocation.

XVIII

The huge melons were split and each of us –
Man and boy – got a whole chilled half with rings
Of black and brown pips set in orange flesh,
Succulent after the desert day.

Were the fruit in fact so large
Or is it that I was small
And he, turning his hemisphere
Between the hands that magicked cape and sword,
Said, 'It's like the Toreo.' 'Look at those dark hats!'
With his knife he scraped them from the heart,
Then gingerly dug out the first, best sweetness.

On the long verandah, after arguments and tall tales,
Away from the sunlight's slow combustion, in the stale
Smoke of cooking fires and men's sweat, evening
Began to imitate the bougainvillea –
The sky bruised, darkened.
It was time then to shower before dinner
And everyone went together, since the last
Were likely to be left soaped when the tank had drained.
I was first and lingered by the skirt of spray
To watch my idols come out of the shadows
And cover their naked skin with a suit of lights.
My world had been of women; here were men,
One man especially, the best matador
I ever saw, an Indian, a god, grown rich,
With an unexpected voice, shrill as a cat's,
A cat's courage and its several lives.

That day with *capote* and *muleta*
It had pleased him to dazzle us. It was a *tienta*
Where they test livestock to see how strong the blood is.
Matadors practise without the need
To kill or count applause, as a virtuoso might
Bow to silence, adjust the stool
And play his best preludes to an empty room.
He dazzled us all the same, we were hoarse with cheering,
Until an enormous creature with splayed horns
Pinned him against a *burladero*,
Kept butting, butting him for a full minute.

We carried him gently, as though an angel had fallen.
'I'm not hurt,' he said. That he had to say it
Meant he was hurting, but it was his business.
We lay him on a bench in the shade and fanned him.
Then he walked off by himself beyond the stables.

'How are you now?' I asked when he came to bathe.
He showed me on the skin the horns' abrasions,
Two long burns like grill-marks scorched on steak.
'A little to either side and the kidneys might have been
Unhappy tonight,' he said, then he showed me over
Each of the twenty scars on calf, thigh, groin.
It was a map, each gore a history. 'And the worst
Was this one,' a little livid ridge, he winced to see it.
I stared, repelled and choked by love, considering
A body wounded and risen from its ashes
Twenty times, to triumphs I had witnessed.
Later I managed to ask, 'Could I be a matador?'
He'd seen my first clumsy cape-work that morning.
'How can I tell? I'd have to study your form. '
Then, because he was an Indian and liked me,
'I doubt it. It isn't in your blood.'

Next day we rode out to the steep grazing,
Chose bulls for the *corrida* at Tijuana.
After that they rounded up three cross-bred calves
And herded them into the ring. 'What for?' 'You'll see.'
They roped and felled them, one at a time, and held
The hind legs wide, slit the scrotums with a razor,
And pressed out pearly, tear-shaped testicles.
The empty bags they tied with string, the bullocks
Struggled to their feet and trotted out.
Hardly a drop of blood on the cowmen's hands.
That night around the fire they cooked and ate,
The firelight's pulse playing on their faces.

A week of those heads crescented with death,
Dancing at you, then away, enraged, their autism
Deceived and punished into art – a week among
Interpreters of peril and cruel grace,
Evenings on the long verandah, under large framed photos
Of famous bulls and fighters, staled adventure:
Once there were many giants, now only one,

Companioned with shadows, ghosts at grass, ghosts
Feebly working beside him with cape and sword.
I had arrived too late at the arena:
My hero was now cheaply garlanded.
Had he died, I would have died, I was sure of that.
Such was the love I had those nights I sat
Beside him, or close at his feet, those days
Riding behind him and his twenty scars.
Now, when I think of him, I don't see his face,
But the livid scar, his worst, that looked like the lid
Of a dead eye. I am repelled
And no less choked by love.

XIX

It was late summer, Friday, four o'clock,
The light-stunned Alameda. He ambled through,
Nodding to the vendors, the corporal,
The sweeper, photographer, the gaudy women.
Of the Spanish exiles I remember only him –
A poet with a king's surname, though he was Republican.
His Christian name was Lion.
King and lion, but a common man:
In my clothing sleeps the dust of every highway
And the sweat of many agonies.
Suddenly he comes upon us, spreads his arms
As if to fly, embraces us, then takes
My father by both hands: 'Don Carlos!'
'You've not met my youngest, León? My second family.'
'I should be so lucky as to have only two!'
He takes my hand more willingly than it's given
And I avert my face, he rests his hand
First on my head and then my shoulder. How
Lightly it weighs, and how lightly he was passing
Along the promenade, looking left and right
For Spain, and his youth, his heart, his fantasy
Of unbribed justice; how very lightly
He flies, as a stone flung from a crater
After the first turbulence flies cooling
Until it could be a bird, and then it falls.

When I visited Segovia years later
I saw a castle like a great ship poised

To sail on air, but made of stone
The way so many dreams translate in stone,
In prose, in blood, in history, and go down.

The weight of his hand, and in rustling sunlight
Their voices – now both dead – talking as friends,
And I never knew
My father had such friends (as when he quoted
Victor Hugo in French, only once in our life
Speaking French, quoting verse, leaving me at a loss
With a stranger I thought I knew, of whom I'm made).

As poet and man he played cleanly,
Without trick or miracle, his seemingly marginal role,
Singing *the Destined Song which the stars won't forget*
And his people will stumble upon, and unearth themselves
In him, as I do when I recollect
That promenade with my father, that hand on my head
Resting as the priest's does on my son's head at the rail;
But we were in bright daylight by the bandstand,
He smoked a cheroot, he did not bless
But attached me by a blighted succession
To a tideless war, to his Troy abandoned by dazed
Warriors with no luggage but their language
And found in exile echo, and its echo.

XX

Lantana clouded a hill in each of your worlds,
Weaving the slope with gritty fibres, giving a blur of hue.
Here in your final world the cluster stars of pink and yellow
Outstay you in their dark of sticky leaves.
The scents cling still of your hair and hands in the room
That speculates on pines and palms, the crazy woodpeckers
Drilling their acorns in and out, a shattering jay.
That speculates alone without your eyes.

Never having shared this house with you
It has become less alien now you've left it.
Like me bereaved, it will revive in time.
The trees will alter, and the shade until
Nothing's quite the same, yet it will retain you
Even when the furniture arranges itself

Around other lives. At least this one wide bedroom
Is yours for good, with its gaze on the steep trees,
The violent mimosa flared at the fence and further
A huge Pacific with two tankers moving
So slowly they'll never get to port.

Calhoun, Capistrano, Coyoacan – together
We left behind so many worlds before I left you,
But never in this way and never again. The brass
Casket of ashes (warm from the sun) we laid
In a box with flowers from your garden, lowered it
On ropes into a hole of statutory depth.
Two bored Chicanos tamped the earth hard, laid the turf
Back over, leaving hardly a scar. Good surgeons!
She is alive. I read the psalm. I feel her pulse.

After twenty years of 'flying visits',
My 'pressing affairs' and 'I can spare about a week',
You're hardly stranger dead than when you lived,
But for this sadness like a fog I can't see through
That will not clear, that rises from your body;
Or a smoke of death, and scentless,
The air of love now visible, milk-white.

If I had heart I'd number all the losses.
It's the real love I wasted. Even when I chose
Exile in resentment it was there. I knew it given
And only death could take it, which it has,
Setting it where it echoes like a call
Morning, evening, now. If I try to walk,
As an infant risks first steps towards coaxing arms,
I fall half way, and take amiss the loving laughter.
Rubbing my eyes I rise and try again.

Note on *The Love of Strangers*

The poems in *The Love of Strangers* are about people – family, writers, artists and others – who stay with me and whose presences I wanted to engage and, as far as possible, to share, while at the same time acknowledging my own perspective on them, keeping as true as I could to the occasions that they gave me.

When *The Love of Strangers* was published in 1989 some critics were irritated that the 'strangers' were not named. The book's title with its quiet polemic was no defence. But if I had called a poem 'Pier Paolo Pasolini', 'Robert Frost' or 'Joselito Huerta', readers might have come at it with their own preconceptions and expectations of the subject. What matters to me is the ways they are in memory – 'truth to the impression', as Ford would have said – even when facts are as specific and accurate as I can make them.

I also felt – and feel – that a degree of discretion is necessary because of the inevitable subjectivity of impressions, and the nature of some of the occasions. It was not a desire to obscure the poems that made me leave the strangers anonymous, but a wish to free them from the sometimes vexed, or harsh, tonalities of their occasions. In any case, the identities can be inferred without much difficulty. In a review in *Agenda*, Donald Davie deduced them all.

The sequence follows a reverse chronology, starting with my father and ending with my mother. As the sequence progresses the 'narrator' regresses to childhood. Those strangers I feel comfortable to name are: V. the poet Janos Pilinsky, VI. the painter David Alfaro Siqueiros (both in any case identified by name in their respective poems), VII. the poet, critic, translator and editor Edgell Rickword, VIII. my nurse Gabina Trigueros, IX. the poet Elizabeth Daryush, Robert Bridges' daughter, XI. Italian poet, novelist, film-maker and polemicist Pier Paolo Pasolini, XII. translator, poet and critic Robert Fitzgerald, XIV. my grandfather Ernest Alfred Schmidt, XV. Robert Frost, XVI. the restorer Jesus Casanova, XVII. the philologist and translator Angel María Garibay, XVIII. my favourite bullfighter of all time Joselito Huerta, and XIX. the exiled Spanish Republican poet León Felipe. For reasons which have nothing to do with the poems themselves, I remain uncomfortable about naming any more, and – respecting this discomfort which has remained constant for eight years – I leave it to the poems to speak them.